The Jou

A Life Journey Through The Eyes Of A Paranoid Schizophrenic

Davina Falcon

chipmunkapublishing
the mental health publisher

Published by
Chipmunkapublishing
PO Box 6872
Brentwood
Essex CM13 1ZT
United Kingdom

http://www.chipmunkapublishing.com

Edited by Sandra Nimako - Boatey

ISBN   978-1-84991-868-8

Chipmunkapublishing   gratefully   acknowledge   the support of Arts Council England.

My Mental Health Experiences

The help received by professionals has varied according to what area I have lived. Basically, when unwell I lose touch with reality, hear voices, feel persecuted and often rant and rave. The help I receive now is great – everyone listens and acts accordingly. I am very satisfied, feel well supported and I am grateful for this. I do not see my illness as a stigma; I feel this is why I stay so well and stable. I also take my medication. If I see it as a stigma, what can I expect from the everyday public? Its just like any illness that can be controlled with drugs.

Mental illness doesn't discriminate against anybody – it could even be you.

The Journey

Here's a story in poem and prose,
let me take you by the nose.
Some is good, some is bad,
some is the best I've ever had.
Life has its ups and downs,
some will even make you frown.
Abuse is there that makes you scared,
hope you are all well prepared.
Through the poems and the prose,
whatever happens nobody knows.
I'll show you the fight that took me through my life,
some is even full Of strife,
but always present is the light.
Even full of bits of spice.
Even skeletons are here and there
that often cause me to despair.
It's all very true and real,
let me take you round the wheel.
Even prison is an issue,
so you may even want a tissue.
Mental illness is a blight in this very fight,
medication helps us through,
what else can we really do?
Here I end the first chapter
what on earth is the matter.
I hope this poem gives you light
and helps you through the lonely nights.

The Abduction

The day I was abducted everyone was looking; I was unaware I should of been scared.

My mum was livid that this should happen in a small village.

They searched high and low, I didn't really know.

This man must of been a con and things must of gone wrong.

He didn't touch me that I know, I told the police, I had to go.

I didn't get the sweets that really made me weep.

My brothers were sad to learn that they left me all alone, they should of taken me with them, I would of been hidden.

What happened to the man I can't understand.

I was back home with my Mam safe and well, hope you are all as well.

Days Out During School Holidays

We had lots of fun once the summer holidays had begun.

We would go on the beach and play in the sand often using just our hands.

We would go swimming in the pool just acting the fool.

We often had a lolly or ice cream while we played rounders on the beach, with rubber sandals on our feet.

My Mum, Gran and Aunty would join in the fun once the day had begun.

It must of cost my mum a lot, as she would treat us quite a lot.

The days we had were full of fun and I often think of my Mum.

My Gran

My Gran lived with me, my Mum and Dad and my brothers.

She had quite a good influence on all of us.

Whilst my parents were at work, my Gran looked after us.

We used to go touring round the Lake District on days out by coach.

We also went to garden parties, which were great fun and very enjoyable.

My Gran became like a second Mum to me and my brothers.

We cared for her a great deal.

Sometimes my Gran took us away on holiday to various places like Ilfracombe, Morecambe and sometimes to her sisters house.

Sometimes the holidays included my Mum and Dad.

Other times, when I was about 14, my mum and dad would go on holiday on their own and I would go away with my Gran.

My Gran was game for anything, such as fishing with my brother - she would put the maggots on the hook and sit patiently waiting to catch fish.

We all cherished my Gran and I often think about her a lot.

A Poem About My Gran

Gran you were lots of fun and was always available and dependable.

You were always there for us and, hopefully, we were there for you.

You gave me lots of your time and patience.

I will always remember you and cherish you.

It was great to have known you and you will never be forgotten.

Hope you found peace and I will see you soon, one day.

My Gambling Problem

It became a compulsion to feed slot machines and I would spend every penny I had, to the extent I would walk home for miles.

I thought 'try another coin I might win.' Then another, then another, but still I didn't win.

The habit had taken over and this went on for several years.

Then one day, I don't know why, but I no longer needed to feed slot machines.

I don't bother with machines or arcades. Why? I don't know.

Dirty Nick

I was too young to know he was grooming me, ready to pounce.

He would throw money to me in small parcels and make sexual gestures and touch me

He taught me exercises to try to make my bust bigger.

It went on for years but started when I was about seven.

I didn't know it was wrong until later.

It has caused me a lot of problems and made me think sex was dirty, something they do to you and a one sided issue.

I am desperately trying to relate to men sexually but it is difficult.

You probably wonder how I deal with it, I deal with it by avoidance, it is the only way.

Also I have often done it for them, but now I don't. I please myself and don't do it at all.

My message for young people is try to get help before it damages your adult life as well.

The Annual Holiday

Every year we go away for a weeks stay.

It was always full of fun and I always enjoyed the run.

The night before, we would be so excited, and once we were there we would be delighted.

One year we went to Pwhellie Butlins, we had half board accomodation. The food was great and we cleared our plate.

We would be in and out of the arcades spending money and having fun, once the holiday had begun.

We would make friends and run and play and enjoy the holiday.

We would swim and dance the days away and be in bed fast asleep ready for the rest of the week.

So mark my words the holiday was good from start to finish and my memories will never diminish.

The Night I Was Raped

The night I was raped I could not escape it was like a burning arrow.

Would I see tomorrow?

All I wanted was a shower, in the very hour.

I felt powerless and scared in the end I despaired.

I had a bath in bleach and looked like a peach.

Who did it, I do not know. It was cold dark and damp and I didn't have a lamp.

It happened in the woods, so fast then it was over at last.

I felt dirty and sore and I knew nobody saw.

In the end I blocked it out.

I think I should of screamed and shouted.

I was fifteen and all alone, I didn't even have a phone.

If this happens to you make sure you tell, so the person goes to hell.

Final Year In School

During my last year at school, I was on mild tranquilliser and feeling down.

I knew it needed to be turned around.

My exams went really well, I passed them all I felt swell.

My mum and dad were very proud and clapped and shouted out loud.

I was suffering from urine incontinence day and night, which made feel a sight.

I had an operation on my bladder which made a slight difference it went on for years

I was often in tears.

My future was in my hands and was the start of my plans.

College was what came next, I wasn't at all perplexed.

The Next Five Years

Once leaving school, I went to college to do a Home Management and Family care course.

I really enjoyed the course and did very well.

In the final year of the course I was offered a job at a Leonard Cheshire home working with the terminally ill.

I spent five years working there enjoyed and gained a lot of good experience.

But with past problems I was often depressed and suicidal.

When I was twenty one I bought a residential caravan which was on a site, six months later it burnt down.

Then I worked alongside of an Occupational Therapist helping make aids for the residents and also doing various activities such as arts and crafts and games.

After five years I left to gain more experience.

From Twenty One To Twenty Nine Years

For the next twelve months I did puppet shows round a city and also art and craft workshops within the community. Which I thoroughly enjoyed, it was very much people friendly.

Circumstances took me away into the countryside which consisted of about ten to fifteen houses.

I was often depressed and lonely spending hours in bed when off work.

At first I had a part-time job in a children's home cleaning then received a full time job in a special care unit which was great and rewarding.

We would take the clients out into the community and generally improve their quality of life.

Some had severe learning difficulties and behaviour problems.

I still felt something was lacking, that being male companionship.

One major improvement in my life was when I was twenty six a neurologist gave me a desmospray for my bladder problem which worked and meant no more wet beds plastic sheets or pads, I was over the moon.

Then I was given a job in a children's home which however I felt I needed more specialist training so after getting several A-levels in history, sociology and psychology I went to university to study a degree in psychology.

Whilst studying I had a nervous breakdown and was diagnosed with Schizo-affective disorder

I thought It was them

I was diagnosed with Schizo affective disorder
I thought it was them.
I was in a secure unit, hearing voices and feeling persecuted.
I thought it was them.
I thought I was God, then Eve.
 I thought it was them.
I thought they were putting people in planes and shooting them.
I thought it was them.
I wouldn't get in my mum's car because it was red and dangerous.
I thought it was them.
I had electric shock treatment.
I knew it wasn't them.

On Discharge From Hospital

After five months in hospital, I got a job working in a hostel as a support officer with people with learning difficulties full time with social services.

About a year later the residents were moved into dispersed housing.

They would run the house like we do, paying bills, buying their own food and generally doing what everybody else does.

Our job was to support them and basically giving them a good quality of life, which I hope we achieved.

The residents excelled and gained more confidence and improved in as much they developed more control over their own life.

Whilst working there I helped to take disabled people on holiday for a company in London, to various destinations like Florida, Hawaii, Malta, Austria.

They would pay for the holiday and give you a hundred pound whether it was a week or more.

It was often hard work and involved twenty four hour care and a lot of lifting, but still it was a lot of fun and good experience.

After this I committed a couple of crimes and whilst waiting to be sentenced I was in prison for nine months and later given a three year probation order, residency order in a bail hostel and a treatment order.

No Place For Me In Society

My emotions were in turmoil and I was full of anxiety, I felt there was no place for me in society.

I committed a couple of crimes in the hope I would serve time and the judge would throw away the key, as I felt there was no place for me in society.

Running away to me is the easiest way of dealing with life's ups and downs, as I felt there was no place for me in society.

My experience of prison was a mixture of solitude, fun, misery, friendship and fights, being told when to eat, drink, go to bed. This did me as there was no place in society for me.

But after months of deliberation and help from several quarters, whom I'm grateful to. Freedom is a blessing and I have now found a place for me in society.

After sentencing

My experience in a bail hostel was an eye opener; many of the women were on the game often to support a drug habit.

I was having counselling, the staff were nice and helpful. One day I was in the red light district and a police man asked me if I was a working girl, I said no I was unemployed they laughed.

After a few months I was moved to another bail hostel which was the best thing that happened, I got a job in a factory and started paying rent.

I was still having counselling and doing well.

After about twelve months I moved back into the community and still progressed and was working.

I bought my own house and had to see a probation officer once a week, plus a community psychiatric nurse, a psychologist and a psychiatrist. They believed in me and I came on in leaps and bounds.

After about ten years the counselling was finished and I had several friends and was well integrated into the community. To this day I'm member of a mind group and on the whole quite content.

However, one night I was mugged, all for twenty pence for a phone call. I found out later, this woman was a drug addict.

She was looking for money and even went in my knickers. She hit me with a bottle three times and I kneed her in the stomach she gave up and ran off.

The laugh of it all was, I had three bumps on my head and two black eyes. I was rushed to hospital with the sirens going, then was left for three hours on a stretcher. I was quite shaken but recovered.

My Companion

My dog is my pride and joy.

She gives me unconditional love and is always there.

My mental health is eased by having my dog.

It gives me something to focus on, nurture and care for.

She is a lot of fun and full of mischief.

She will dig in the garden and her snout will be covered in mud.

She is comical.

If ever I'm feeling delicate, myself and the dog will go on a walk round the country side which is a good form of distraction away from upsetting issues.

When I come home she welcomes me wagging her tail.

She is lovely.

I would recommend a pet for anyone as they give you company, joy and are a calming influence.

My dog is very clean and not at all destructive.

When I go to my Mums, the dog comes with me.

Its quite a long journey and she spends her time looking out of the window or searching for leftovers.

She is very well behaved on the journey and is often exhausted at the end of it.

My West Island Terrier

When I am happy, you are there.

When I am sad, you are there.

When I am angry, you are there.

When I am stressed, you are there

In fact when I am anything, you are there.

That is why I care.

My parents

My parents have always done the best for us all.

We are quite a close family unit.

We are always there for each other.

If you kick one of us, you kick us all.

My Dad was frightened when I became unwell with a mental illness, he never came to visit me in hospital.

Yet, he would come to visit me when I was in prison, every fortnight.

However, prison could have been avoided if the psychiatrist had listened to me and acted accordingly.

His response was, "it will cost a lot of money and take a long time."

Well – it certainly cost more than they bargained for.

Despite all this, my parents stood by me and were a power of strength and I will never forget what they did and what they sacrificed.

My Mum and Dad are proud of me now and are happy that I am content.

Mum and Dad

Mum and Dad you are always there, I do believe you really care.

You have stood by me through thick and thin.

And always, let me come in.

I love you loads you have always helped me on the roads.

If I can help you I will, cause I think you are both swell.

I will try to remain content and never treat you with contempt.

Through To The Present Day

Although I still can't cope with men, my life is quite fulfilling.

I had a job as a supportive permitted worker but due to government cutbacks was   made redundant. What is laughable is now they are moaning because disabled people are not working, but it's their fault.

I now keep myself busy doing various voluntary work like helping with an art and craft group and a table top unit and learning more skills to get back in employment .

One point I would like to make is it's important to listen, but also to act as actions speak louder than words.

If people years ago would have acted, a lot of my problems would have been avoided and saved a lot of money

However I now receive a lot of help and people listen and act accordingly.

The Mind Group

National Mind is a charity for people who are suffering from mental illness.

When I moved into this area, obviously I knew nobody.

The Mind group helped me integrate into the community and meet new people which was invaluable.

The Mind group has been a pillar of support alongside other agencies.

Where it is based, is in a type of shopping centre which means you have to mix with the general public, which in my opinion is a good thing.

Hopefully it will put stigma into perspective and make people realise that we are not mad axe men. I hope it will make them understand, that most of us are more likely to harm ourselves as opposed to anyone else.

We go out on trips and gather socially and discuss issues, receive support and support each other.

I have made many good friends and one person in particular who is disabled physically and also suffers from mental illness, but we go out as friends not carers.

My friend takes care of her own transactions and we have a mutual agreement on what we do.

It is not a one-sided issue, we support each other.

We go on holiday together and have a great deal of fun.

Our friendship is as great now as when we first met.

Consequently, the Mind group is part of my life and support network.

I just go when I want to.

My success story

I would like to say to all the people who have helped me since prison - thank you.

I can now manage my day to day routines and feel quite content.

Many people have helped me along the way and this book is dedicated to those people, including family and friends.

I hope this book gives you a feeling of hope and inspiration.

However, I have been lucky and the judge that dealt with my case saw my case as a cry for help.

I don't recommend getting help through this same way, but do try and get help as there are many charitable organisations out there such as Survive.

To young people I would say if the help is offered, take it and ensure your adult life isn't affected by any childhood issues.

I realise it can be upsetting but if treated correctly can make a huge difference to your future, especially if its delivered gradually.

It took me ten years of counselling but I have finally arrived at the end and can honestly say, life has treated me great and I have finally found happiness despite a couple of unresolved issues.

I am having counselling again but this is to manage my negative thought pattern and is quite successful. It's learning to normalise your thoughts and put things into perspective. It also involves using several distraction techniques.

My problems were made worse because of my mental health issues, but I've learnt to live with them and accept my illness. It is just like someone with epilepsy which can be controlled by drugs.

I do not feel mental illness is a stigma as it can happen to anybody including you.

Ending Message

My life is great and full of fun, I really do believe I've won.

If you let them get you down you may as well be underground.

These words I speak every week, to remind me I'm not that weak.

Mark my words it's been an up-hill struggle but I no longer see a muddle.

I see a life full of spice.

So no matter what, make the most of what you've got.

The Journey

Lightning Source UK Ltd.
Milton Keynes UK
UKOW040509181012

200727UK00001B/11/P